I'm Single. Now What?
13 Steps on How to Live Single and Free

MICHELLE G. CAMERON

I'M SINGLE: NOW WHAT? 13 STEPS ON HOW TO LIVE SINGLE AND FREE
Copyright © 2014 by Michelle G. Cameron
All rights reserved.

Published by:
NyreePress Literary Group
P.O. Box 164882
Fort Worth, TX 76161
www.nyreepress.com

All rights reserved. No part of this book may be used or reproduced by any means, graphic, electronic, or mechanical, including photocopying, recording, taping or by any information storage retrieval system without the written permission of the publisher. Copying this book is both illegal and unethical.

ISBN print: 978-0-9903486-6-5
ISBN e-book: 978-0-9906662-7-1
Library of Congress Catalog Control Number: 2014949178

Christian Living / Relationships / Inspirational

Printed in the United States of America

NYREEPRESS

I'm SINGLE.
NOW WHAT?
13 Steps on How to Live Single and Free

MICHELLE G. CAMERON

Acknowledgements

Book cover design – Ellis & Ellis Consulting Group, LLC (Paul K Ellis)
Photography – Zion Images (Wardell Duncan)
Makeup – Blaq Glamour House (Sheena Cherilus)
Hair – 3H Precision Barbers & Stylists (Kevin Hudson)
Styling – From the SolesUp Styling and Image Consulting (Fania Golding Beck)
Jewelry – An Extra Touch (Kakila Hunter)

Book Reviews

"When communicating with a generation that requires information as quickly as possible, practicality is the key to effectiveness. This guide goes beyond words for the individual that really wants to effectively understand and explore the challenges of single life. With each chapter, you will walk away evaluating critical parts of your heart and life that will assist you at arriving at a place of wholeness and freedom. This guide focuses on many of the prevalent thoughts and questions for singles and will help you to capture the answers you need to live single, saved, and satisfied while waiting for your mate to come. "

LaBryant Friend (@labryantfriend)
Senior Pastor, Mount Calvary M.B. Church, Tucson, AZ
Author, "Daddy, Daughters, and Devotions"

"The older I get and the more aware of who I am and what I ultimately aspire to get from life; I seem to understand singleness better by the day. It is far more than just a status. It is deeper than holding out and waiting on "the one." There is more to it than merely striving to conquer the overwhelming feelings of being alone, or feeling unwanted.

Singleness is a process; a challenge; and a time span that involves a variety of defining moments. Most literally, it can make or break you, in a number of ways, if you are devoid of a survival method that works. Therefore, in order to maneuver through this period successfully, assistance is required. But not just any assistance. You need the type of assistance offered by Michelle Cameron in her manual for singles-- I'm Single. Now What?

Without doubt, this manual will be resourceful in providing sensible, precise, and necessary information and methods. Peeling off the layers and boldly addressing aspects of singleness that are often shunned or downplayed by the masses, Michelle has published a "must-have" book for all individuals that are presently single.

The struggle is real; but with this book, it has to become better and bearable."

Khas Dock (@khasdock)
Author, "Shades of Grace"

"Every once in a while, there is book that comes along that grabs your full attention because you know it's truly written from the heart of someone with personal experience. Minister Michelle Cameron hits the proverbial "nail on the head," with her amazing book, "I'm Single, Now What." Of the many things I appreciate about this book and Minister Cameron's ministry to Singles, is that she takes the negative shade that is often thrown on being single and allows the reader to examine singleness through the balanced lens of God's Word, and a single life lived. With the majority of our local churches predominantly single, this book is long overdue in helping singles to understand that their lives have meaning, value and worth that extends well beyond the validation of marriage that many people feel they need. Thank God for this needed, bold and courageous writing that is sure to feed your soul, ready your spirit, and challenge you to live life to the fullest. This is truly "a manual on how to live single and free!"'

Bishop Kenneth M. Yelverton (@KenYelverton)
Pastor, The Temple of Refuge
Charlotte, North Carolina
Author, "Sex and the Kingdom: A Biblical Portrait of Human Sexuality"

Foreword

MICHELLE CAMERON IS A NAME I HEARD very clearly one afternoon. I was sitting in my office praying that God would send the right person for the task at hand. The task was the resurrection of our singles ministry after a far-too-long hiatus. What ministry to singles meant ten years prior was not exactly what was present at that moment in time in our church. In addition to those who had never married, there were men and women of all ages who were divorced, single with children, or widowed; and there was a growing population of individuals who were deciding to be single for life—all seeking ministry for singles.

This changing face of the Christian single life meant that our approach to ministry also had to change. The approach to ministering to this population needed to be multi-faceted—more than a place to meet a potential mate and prepare for marriage. It needed to be a training ground for maximizing the single life in order to become all that God had designed singles to be no matter what the future held concerning their marital status. The complexity of this assignment meant the person at the helm would have to be divinely called to this kind of work. The person would also have to share the heart of God concerning the single life. Michelle Cameron is the name God spoke very clearly to me that afternoon.

What you hold in your hand is evidence of her call to this ministry and the fact that her heart beats in unison with God's concerning singles. Drawing from personal experiences and careful research, Michelle candidly, thoughtfully, and clearly presents us with a wonderful balance of the spiritual and practical tools necessary to live single and free. So find your favorite relaxation spot, curl up there, and enjoy the journey on your own or gather a group of friends and embark on the journey in community. You can even go about this journey with the singles ministry in your local congregation. However you decide to journey toward living single and free, with each section of this book, you will be encouraged and better equipped because you did.

The Reverend Dr. Danielle L. Brown
Pastor of Church Life
Cathedral International (The Historic Second Baptist Church)
Perth Amboy, New Jersey

Dedication

I want to dedicate this book to every unmarried person who may feel alone and discouraged. **This book was written just for YOU.** I am walking this single journey with you now, and I understand how it feels; but I can also testify to the awesomeness of God and how He can turn difficult challenges into wonderful testimonies! Be encouraged. God is still with you, and He longs to wrap you in His arms. I pray that this book ministers to you.

Why I Wrote This Book

I HAVE BEEN LEADING OUR LOCAL Singles Ministry for 2 years, and I have had several conversations in person and online with discouraged singles. Some have almost reached a standstill. Yet, there are many who are successfully moving forward with their lives, and are enjoying every moment.

Whether you are discouraged, taking life by the horns and living your dream or somewhere in-between, I want this book to be an arm around your shoulders. I know personally what it is like to be at every stage, and I want you to know that you will be okay. Read this book with an open mind to learn, and use the valuable information presented here to put some things in place that may not yet be there.

See this book as a companion throughout your single journey.

Note that some of the topics may apply to anyone, but my desire was for you to have all the topics you need to review in one resource.

Refer to this book often, and recommend it to others.

We as singles have so much to offer. Believe me when I say this: Together we can change the world!

Table of Contents

Chapter 1: *I'm Single. Now What?* 14
Chapter 2: *Single with Soul Ties* 16
Chapter 3: *Singles and Dating: The Sex Struggle* 20
Chapter 4: *Singles and Friendships with the Opposite Sex.* 26
Chapter 5: *Singles and Health (with Mr. Joshua Smith)* 30
Chapter 6: *Singles and Finances (with Mr. Kenny Pugh)* 37
Chapter 7: *Raising Children while Single (with Mr. Billie Miller)* 48
Chapter 8: *Singles Walking into Destiny by Living Intentionally* 58
Chapter 9: *Singles and Mentors* 64
Chapter 10: *Singles Preparing for Marriage* 69
Chapter 11: *Single By Choice* 72
Chapter 12: *What Not to Say to Singles* 76
Chapter 13: *Single over the Holidays* 79
Single and Free! Final Words 82
Singles – Questions for Reflection 86
Social Media Quotes for Singles 89

I'm Single. Now What?

I'VE BEEN SINGLE FOR MOST OF MY LIFE. I was single until the age of twenty-five, when I got married as a virgin. Through circumstances discussed in my first book, *It's My Life and I Live Here: One Woman's Story*, I became single again nine and a half years later, but this time with a son. My marriage, which I had hoped would last forever, had to end because of repeated instances of infidelity and verbal/mental abuse. After it ended I used to wonder what would happen next.

For me, the last nine years have been a whirlwind of non-stop action. From starting and completing my MBA, to publishing my first book, to becoming a licensed minister, to my appointment as a singles ministry leader, to owning a home and burying my beloved grandmother—all while raising a boy and working full time outside of the home; the twists and turns could not be predicted.

If you've always been single, or if you're single again, let us take this journey together. There will be unexpected twists and turns, and many highs with some lows. Allow God to walk with you as you journey through this season of your life. If you have decided to stay with the single journey for a season or for the rest of your life, it is my hope that it will be a time of deep introspection and personal growth filled with love and laughter. You may cry sometimes or feel lonely, but be assured that you are not taking this journey alone.

Feel free to review this book many times during your journey and refer it to others who may be taking this path too.

Single with Soul Ties

WHAT IS A SOUL TIE? The Online Urban Dictionary defines a soul tie as, *"A spiritual/emotional connection you have to someone after being intimate with them, usually engaging in sexual intercourse. To the point that when you want to be rid of them from your mind and your life, even when you are far away from them and out of their presence you still feel as if they are a part of you and a part of you is with them, causing you to feel unwhole, as if you've given up some of yourself intangible that cannot be easily possessed again."*

Soul ties are prevalent in the single population. Soul ties from the past may be the reason why some singles are always moving from one new relationship to the next.

As singles attempt to move on romantically, the invisible chains of previous soul connections tend to bind their hearts. Soul ties prevent us from becoming 100% vested in our next relationship, and this includes marriage. How can this prevalent issue be solved?

1. First, we must admit that soul ties exist and that we may have at least one. Many people may not be aware that they are still connected to someone and may not recognize all the signs. Here are some of them:
    a. You are unable to release someone with whom you no longer have a relationship. You feel "stuck," as if your life is empty or meaningless without that person.
    b. You cannot let go of their phone number or a personal item of theirs (a shirt, a baseball cap, etc.)
    c. You are always wondering what they are up to and if they have moved on to someone else.

d. You stalk their social media pages to keep up with what they are doing with their lives.
e. You make efforts to stay in touch with them or with others who are close to them to gain information.
f. You daydream or reminisce of times you shared together and may wonder if it's possible to get back together.
g. You are not open to new relationships or friendships with the opposite sex.
h. You have many dreams about them, including sexual dreams.

2. Next, we must be willing to leave the past in the past. Are you ready to delete phone numbers, get rid of personal effects, and resist the urge to stalk them?

3. Pray and fast. Renounce the spiritual connections that you still have with the individual(s). Allow God to move into the depths of your heart and spirit to uproot the feelings and urges.

4. Consider seeking professional help through a mental health professional. You may need to sit and talk it out regularly with a trained person who can help you sort out your feelings.

5. Realize that you may not be able to release someone immediately, especially if they meant a lot to you or were a part of your life for many years.

Be honest with yourself. Personal honesty helps you start the journey to personal healing and development. Facing who we really are and unmasking our hearts is something that many singles may not feel ready to do. Consider this: When you are completely healed of soul ties, freedom will be yours to enjoy!

Singles and Dating:
The Sex Struggle

IF MOST SINGLES ARE HONEST, dating and sex have been almost synonymous for most of their lives. The typical scenario may include a first encounter at a party, Happy Hour, or some other location, followed by an exchange of phone numbers for hours of talk, then possibly a couple outings and then—sex.

If the single is in church or in ministry, the struggle with having sex or being surrounded by sex is compounded by feelings of guilt and helplessness. The emphasis on sex in the media cannot be understated. Most singles can verify that they were exposed to sex at an early age, whether it was through molestation/abuse or seeing it in magazines or on TV. The younger generation of singles (ages twenty to thirty) may not remember when they did *not* know what sex was.

Here are some questions to ask yourself as you think on this topic:

1. Do you believe that it is possible to date without being sexually active?

2. Is it healthy to become sexually involved with every person that you date?

3. Even with careful (and religious) birth control use, is having sex outside of the confines of marriage safe?

4. If you never marry, could you live without having sex?

Personally, I believe in sex within the confines of marriage, as stated in the Bible (Colossians 3:5-8, The Message: "And that means killing off everything connected with that way of death: sexual promiscuity, impurity, lust, doing whatever you feel like whenever you feel like it, and grabbing whatever attracts your fancy. That's a life shaped by things and feelings instead of by God. It's because of this kind of thing that God is about to explode in anger. It wasn't long ago that you were doing all that stuff and not knowing any better. But you know better now, so make sure it's all gone for good: bad temper, irritability, meanness, profanity, dirty talk).

When the Scriptures were written, the people hearing them were accustomed to going to the goddess temple to worship via temple prostitutes, so sex played a very important part in their daily activities, possibly even more than it does in many of our lives today. So telling someone who made sacrifices to their gods then slept with temple prostitutes that the practice was sinful meant that they needed a significant spiritual, mental, and emotional transformation to live the new life. Self-control had to become something that they desired and adopted. By allowing the Holy Spirit to be their guide and mentor (along with teachings from Paul and others), they were able to embrace the standards according to God's Word.

Sex does not have to come into the equation in dating, especially if you plan ahead on how to navigate your love life.

Here are a few recommendations you can use as you prepare to live a life that honors God:

1. Pray and seek God's approval before approaching someone of the opposite sex.

This step can save you from tremendous regret and heartache later.

2. Allow God to speak to your heart on saving sex for the covenant of marriage. Keep your heart open to the nudging from the Holy Spirit as He directs your thoughts and actions. This includes involvement with pornography and masturbation.

3. Choose to date someone with the same sexual goal as you. That goal should be to abstain until marriage. This makes it easier, as you can hold each other accountable to keep this commitment.

4. Find a mentor. This must be someone you can trust with intimate details of your life and who will hold you accountable. Inform them when you go out on dates and when you plan to return.

5. Keep dates during the daytime if possible and avoid visiting each other's homes when no one else will be there.

6. Choose dates where you spend time with others around, but you are still able to have

private conversations—such as parks, museums, cafes, and so on.

7. Be intentional. Don't lead each other on or tempt each other to see how much you can get away with and not have sex. It's like playing with fire.

8. Don't go out on a date when you feel like having sex. It's okay to reschedule the date to a day when your hormones are a lot calmer.

9. Consider double dating or going on group dates. These can be options for a more relaxed (and safer) environment to get to know each other better. You will also get to see how the other person interacts with others in a fun group setting.

10. This may be old school, but consider having a chaperone to keep things in check. If you are strongly attracted to each other, it can be easy to go past your convictions in the heat of the moment.

11. If you fall down in the area of sex, consider taking a break from each other to regroup. Pray, fast, and seek godly counsel before spending alone time again with the person.

12. As the relationship develops, consider pre-engagement counseling. This will help both individuals begin to prepare for a significant life change if all goes well.

13. If pre-engagement/pre-marital counseling has given both of you the green light, consider moving up your wedding date.

14. Keep praying for each other and ask God to give you both the strength to stay focused on your goal.

The popular phrase "The struggle is real" definitely applies to dating and sex with singles. Although it is a struggle, the effort to do things God's way are always richly rewarded.

Don't give up!

Singles and Friendships with the Opposite Sex

IS THERE ANYTHING WRONG WITH SINGLES becoming friends with the opposite sex? Some may say it's no big deal. But can any single become friends with someone of the opposite sex with no intentions or expectations? We'll explore this question in this chapter.

First, I am against intimate, opposite-sex friendships with married people, especially if you are not friends with their spouses. Sometimes in business settings opposite-sex friendships with married people may occur, and when I am in those instances I make an effort to ask about their spouse in conversations and greet her appropriately when I see them together. Conversations are free of innuendo, and any statements that can have double meanings are quickly clarified from my end. (I have married male friends who can testify to this.)

So what if your opposite-sex friend is single? Isn't it fair game? Aren't you free to explore every way in which this friendship can go?

First, I believe in getting to know people, especially their character, first. I've been alive long enough to know that reputations are based on appearances but not always based on facts. I take my time in getting to know men. I do not typically open my life to them quickly, because I need to know if I can trust someone first. So my first question is "Can you be trusted?"

After spending some time around him (in group settings where we are both comfortable), I may check up or ask people I trust what their impressions of this person are. Please note that I am not necessarily trying to or planning to date him, but I want to be sure that I am not opening up myself to a charlatan or to someone who may try to take advantage of me.

My next step is to build a meaningful relationship based on mutual interests. My typical mode of action is to avoid one-on-one interaction with men whom I am not dating. This became even more important to me since my recent elevation as a licensed minister, because I want to be considerate of how things may appear to onlookers as well.

After we have built a solid friendship and a shift begins to occur, I have some decisions to make. Do I see this friendship as a possible relationship? Are we pursuing the same purpose? Are we heading in the same direction? Do I feel comfortable with this person representing me as my spouse, should that occur? Are my mentors okay with it should that possibility occur?

Ladies should never make the first move in initiating a relationship, but they should provide space for it to happen. The gentleman should feel that he has been invited into the lady's space and that his request to take it to the next level would be a welcome gesture from her perspective. If the friendship moves into a relationship, it is important to maintain self-respect and self-discipline. When someone respects himself or herself, it is easier for the other person to respect them. If the friendship remains just a friendship (with no movement into a relationship), be classy about it. Realize that everyone is free to choose who they want to have a relationship with, and many times their rejection serves as an open door to another person who sees your worth and does not want to live without you.

Many have testified of friendships with the opposite sex being just that—a friendship—and it may be possible. Just keep in mind that the other person may secretly want the friendship to move to the next level. If you suspect that your friend may desire to take the friendship to the next level, prayerfully consider if this person could be "the one" for you. Many strong friendships have blossomed into beautiful life-long marriages.

If you are friends with someone of the opposite sex and get into a relationship with someone else, realize that some friction that may occur. Some opposite-sex friends may be able to handle you dating, but others may not like that they will have to share you with your special someone. Also be aware that your new beau may not be too excited about your opposite-sex friendships.

If you are serious about your new relationship, initiate a frank discussion on this topic with both of them (separately) to gain their perspective. Your date may be open-minded enough to not feel threatened by opposite-sex friends, but they may not want to handle that scenario. Determine if you are willing to modify your friendships to accommodate a romantic relationship and manage the situation accordingly.

Singles and Health
(with Joshua P. Smith)

NOW, MORE THAN EVER BEFORE, many singles are focusing on health and wellness and are placing a high priority on exercise and eating well. As we prepare ourselves for future relationships and the possibility of marriage, we want to look and feel our best at all times. Even if marriage is not a priority, making significant steps towards healthier lifestyles gives us the ability to do the things we want to do for much longer. In this chapter we will explore several areas concerning health that we can focus on more as singles.

With the onslaught of social media and advanced technology, we are able to self-diagnose some of our symptoms or review advice that may not be credible. Never underestimate the need to have a primary physician as your go-to person to keep up with your health. With one doctor or doctor's office maintaining your health records, it becomes easier to treat or catch adverse situations at an earlier time.

Annual checkups, especially tests based on age, are not to be overlooked. Mammograms for women at age forty (or younger for individuals with primary family members who had cancer), annual Pap smear exams, as well as tests for colon cancer and prostate cancer are very important and should not be postponed. Sometimes these tests may mean the difference between a long, healthy life and imminent death.

Aside from regular checkups and tests, consider daily life choices. Are you eating as healthily as your budget permits? Are you exercising regularly? (I am guilty in this area.) How about your intake of water? Sometimes we fall into a rut with eating habits and over time realize that we've developed health issues related to eating: high cholesterol, high blood pressure, diabetes, and so on. Some of these diseases have a genetic element, but many are brought on by eating too much of what we do not need or too little of what our bodies need. Become familiar with portion sizes of foods that are healthy. It's the other foods we need to be concerned about. Meat intake should be managed, and red meat should be eaten about once a week. Shellfish is high in cholesterol and should be taken in moderation.

Some fish, mainly "meaty" fish, tend to contain mercury. For this reason, eat fish in moderation.

The juicing trend has taken the nation by storm! I think it is a brilliant idea to blend fresh fruit and veggies high in nutrients and fiber together to create a refreshing, healthy, and filling smoothie for optimal benefits! Stories of feeling full for long periods (which then amounts to lower intake of calories and significant weight loss), higher energy levels, enhanced complexion, and healthy, shiny hair and nails are all great benefits. I am also certain that many diseases are being kept at bay by this wonderful phenomenon. There are many recipes available for us to try, so let's get to juicing!

Another aspect of health that is sometimes ignored or kept quiet is mental or psychological health. Depression, bipolar disorder, schizophrenic disorders, and so on are real illnesses. Just like you would see a doctor for diabetic treatment, we need help when our minds or emotions are not working as they should. Some of the deficiencies are biochemical and cannot be prevented. Others are seasonal, like S.A.D. (seasonal affective disorder), or related to an event or tragedy (like 9-11 or the death of a loved one). Regardless of the situation, please get help. If you have a loved one who appears to be unable to cope with typical life situations or who seems to be withdrawn, confused, or sad all the time, offer to take them to get help. They may need to see a psychotherapist or psychiatrist. Prescriptions are also available to help those with mental health issues get back on track and live normal, productive lives.

The stigma attached to getting medical help for mental health issues is significant, especially in African American communities. Fear of being ridiculed, ostracized, or labeled seems to be greater than the opportunity to live a relatively normal life. Let us push aside the stigmas that others want to place on mental issues and get free! Help is available. Sometimes getting help is the difference between living a happy, productive life and living with a cloud hanging overhead that pushes some to commit suicide or other violent acts.

Let's hear what **Joshua P. Smith**, a licensed mental health professional, has to say regarding mental health:

When thinking in terms of being single and whole, it is impossible to leave health out of the equation. Health is divided into three basic dimensions: physical, spiritual, and mental (emotional). It is very possible to be healed in one area and not healed in another area. The combination of the three makes one whole. The enemy's job is to sift us, as Jesus warned Simon Peter in Luke 22:31. To sift means to separate. When we are healed in one area and impaired in another area, we have been sifted, or separated, making us unstable.

One of the most ignored dimensions of health, especially in religious circles, is mental and emotional health. For years, psychology (the study of the soul) has been unwelcomed in our churches because of misconceptions and a lack of understanding. Some circles have even passed on erroneous teaching that mental diseases and disorders do not affect us because of our religious beliefs or our connection with God. My response to that is always the same, "Do Christians get cancer?" Sure they do!

When someone is physically ill, we encourage them to seek professional help. This is not always true when it comes to mental problems. Just like physical sicknesses and ailments touch the body, mental and emotional problems can plague the mind, especially if they are left unchecked.

We must become stewards over our mental and emotional health, just as we are stewards over our physical health. For a long time, the church in general has told us to simply "pray about" mental and emotional problems. However, just as God has given medical doctors and nurses the expertise to deal with our physical ailments, He has also equipped psychiatrists and therapists to help us with our emotional problems.

Proverbs 11:14 says that there is safety in a multitude of counselors. God has gifted individuals with the ability to help you through life's transitions, and there are many counselors who share your same religious and spiritual beliefs. Many of the skills and principles taught even in secular settings come directly from the word of God and are being used to the benefit of unbelievers.

Being assessed or treated for a mental condition does not mean that you do not have faith. It actually means that you are adding works to your faith. There are some mental illnesses that are stress related and can easily worked out in therapy. There are also some mental illnesses that are hereditary, just like there are some physical illnesses that are hereditary. Knowing your family's history will help you watch for warning signs and live a healthy life.

Mental illness is no longer a problem that we can ignore, especially in the church. If you want to not only be healed but also whole, maintain all three dimensions of health. What would it profit you to gain the world and lose your mind [soul]? (Mark 8:36)

For a photo and biography of Joshua Smith, refer to the Appendix.

Let us make our health—all aspects of our health—a priority for ourselves starting TODAY!

Singles and Finances
(with Mr. Kenny Pugh)

TYPICALLY, SINGLES WITHOUT CHILDREN have more disposable income (after student loans!). This is truer of older singles vs. singles who may be just leaving college—unless they landed their dream job directly out of college.

On the other end of the spectrum, single mothers with multiple children typically have less income to go around, and many are living in poverty (Rank, M. R. (2011, Spring).

Wherever you fall within the spectrum, singles need to consider the type of financial future they want to have as they get older. This is true whether marriage occurs or not. Debt elimination and limiting debt accumulation is an area where many singles (and in fact, almost anyone) need discipline.

I will share my personal story here. When I was single (before marriage) I was not careful in spending or saving. I was in significant consumer debt before the age of 25 with very little savings. Those habits did not change overnight when I got married. I firmly believe that when we practice better discipline in finances without a spouse (or without children), it becomes easier to manage financial responsibilities if marriage and a family are desired in the future. Money management is good for everyone at every stage of life.

I asked **Mr. Kenny Pugh**, financial expert, to share some tips to help us as singles.

Financial Tips for Singles from Kenny Pugh

There are many areas to focus on during your season of singleness. Financial preparation is undoubtedly one of these key areas. According to a number of surveys, finances are consistently one of the top reasons cited for couples making the decision to divorce. This means gaining a healthy level of financial responsibility and aptitude is very important to maintaining a level of harmony within marriage, if desired (Scott, S. B., Rhoades, G. K.,

Stanley, S. M., Allen, E. S., & Markman, H. J. (2013). Reasons for divorce and recollections of premarital intervention: Implications for improving relationship education. *Couple and Family Psychology: Research and Practice,* 2(2), 131-145. doi:http://dx.doi.org/10.1037/a0032025).

Fortunately, financial knowledge is a transferable skill that you can learn as a single person. I repeatedly encourage singles to go through the learning process of money basics with the understanding that this will assist you now and in marriage, if desired.

Do you have to become a financial expert? Absolutely not! However, it is important for you to gain a basic comprehensive understanding of money, budgets, debt, financial planning, and financial protection.

Let's take a quick look at each of these…

Budgets

Many of my students can tell you how much of an advocate I am for creating and maintaining a budget. Budgets are simply tools to assist you with establishing a working spending plan. The fluidity of everyday life makes it very difficult to keep track of your finances. However, a budget allows you a working plan for managing your finances.

Creating a budget is the most basic step in allowing your money to work for you. Budgets allow you to understand how your income and expenses work together within a given time period, generally tracked monthly. Unfortunately, people don't realize they're spending more money than they're making until it's too late.

Budgets are like snowflakes in that every one is different. However, the culprits for the demise of people's finances are credit cards and loans. Budgets allow you to be proactive in how you allocate your money, thus placing you in better control of your money. Otherwise, your money is in total control of you.

A good budget provides a one-stop view of how your money is spent. It includes various categories that are customizable to fit your personal needs. Sample categories include rent, mortgage, credit cards, student loans, utilities, and automobile loans.

Don't allow budgeting to be a chore, but look at it as a personal aide in your financial future.

Debt Elimination

Debt elimination is generally a great area to target during your season of singleness. Unfortunately, it is a frustrating area to deal. Don't be discouraged, though; for those who desire marriage, your future spouse will appreciate any progress you can make in paying down any of your outstanding debts. I've never heard of anyone being rejected because they have eliminated their debt.

Debt elimination is a matter of planning, prioritization, and progress. Using the information gathered in the budgeting section of this chapter, you can determine how much extra money you have available to pay down debt (PLAN). Taking inventory of *all* your outstanding obligations (e.g., loans, credit cards) allows you to order how you eliminate your debt (PRIORITIZE). Taking the budget information and inventory of your outstanding debt allows you to begin making progress toward eliminating your debt.

There are generally two approaches to debt elimination. The first is paying off your debt from the highest interest rate to the lowest interest rate. Taking this approach allows you get rid of your high interest obligations first. The second approach is paying your debt off from lowest balance to highest balance. People often opt for this approach because it gives you an opportunity to make progress faster, resulting in a confidence boost in making progress according to your plan.

Debt elimination is a great way to free up your time and resources so you can focus on living your life versus working to pay bills.

Financial Planning (Saving/Investing)

Without a financial plan for saving and investing your money, your chances of saving enough money to achieve your long-term financial goals are slim to none. Saving money is an intentional decision made by conscious people. Saving money requires discipline, sacrifice, and financial understanding.

Dedicated savers buy smart, minimize expenses, plan effectively, and educate themselves on financial concepts. Your single season is a great time to devote toward learning how to save. This doesn't mean you have to become depressed if you are not on your way to saving a million dollars by the end of the year. However, every dollar counts and it's important to begin *today* even if it means only saving twenty dollars per month. A great way to initiate your savings is by setting up a separate account and automating regular deposits into the account.

Saving money in association with the magic of compounding interest is a formula for success. Are you dedicated to applying this principle to your life?

One of the first goals you should set when creating a financial plan is to build an emergency fund. Depending on which financial advisor you listen to, this amount can vary from as little as one thousand dollars to as much as eight to twelve months' worth of expenses. I encourage you to start small and build your way up over time.

As you save money, you'll realize that leaving money in an account bearing less than 1 percent in interest isn't necessarily the best option. This is where investing comes into play. Investing your money is the process of allocating your money with the intent of obtaining the largest return on investment available based on investment type.

It's impossible to address the various investment options in a single chapter. However, I recommend you perform independent research on stocks, bonds, and mutual funds.

Financial Protection (Life Insurance)

No one enjoys discussing the topics of injuries/death. However, it is essential that you take time to ensure you, your family, and assets are protected in the event that injury or death takes place.

Insurance protects your assets against losses that could impact your financial future. This includes your income, home, or automobile(s), etc. People often select insurance as the instrument that protects against adverse situations of life.

Once again, I'm not able to address the details of insurance in a single chapter. However, you can perform independent research on whole life, term life, and universal life insurance.

Term life is insurance that provides a predetermined death benefit if you die within the term covered. However, it doesn't build up any cash benefit during your lifetime.

Whole life is a combination of insurance coverage and investment tool. Your monthly or annual premium goes toward insurance coverage, cash value, and fees.

Variable life is a policy giving you some choice in where your investment is placed. With variable life, the amount of your insurance coverage shifts depending on how the investment portion is doing.

Summary

As a single person, you have a great opportunity to work on your finances without the complexity of having a spouse. Why not take advantage of this opportunity? I promise you will appreciate taking steps to improve your financial future. Not only will you appreciate seizing the opportunity, but your future spouse and family will too.

For a photo and biography of Kenny Pugh, refer to the Appendix.

My question to you:

What are YOU willing to do to get free financially?

Let's kill the bondage of fear by eliminating debt!

Raising Children when Single
(with Mr. Billie Miller)

I AM THE SINGLE MOTHER OF A PRE-TEEN boy, whom I have raised alone since he was a toddler. His father is significantly involved in his life, which I believe is a blessing for him. Becoming a single parent can be a difficult situation, especially in my case where the transition from being a married parent took place.

In single parenting, the feelings of inadequacy are multiplied significantly, especially when faced with decisions or circumstances that typically require at least two adults to handle. Sick days are still one of the biggest challenges in a single-parent home. There is no "back-up" in the home to take care of the children when the parent is sick. And when the children are sick, the parent is usually grounded as well. Parents of children with chronic health situations typically end up finding creative ways to finance their lives, as a typical 9-5 becomes impossible to keep.

Single parents tend to be very independent and hate asking for help. My years of experience have taught me that asking for help is not a sign of weakness. When your family suffers because of your independence, we call that pride. Children of single parent homes need to know that they have someone else the family can run to in times of distress or for just a change in scenery.

I recall when Hurricane Sandy came through our area in late October to early November 2012, and trees pulled power lines down. It was cold, and we were running out of options as the days passed. Food was scarce because stores could not get deliveries. Gas for automobiles was hard to acquire for the same reason—gas deliveries could not get to the stations. Gas had to be rationed, and we had to find creative ways to get something to eat.

As day four came without relief, we got a message to come for breakfast from a friend who had electricity and plenty of food. We went, and my son also had a chance to go and stay with the other side of his family. What a welcome break from our situation!

Single parents, find friends who will love and look out for you and your children. Whenever you can return the favor, do so, but understand that real love doesn't keep records of who did what, when. We help because we love each other and want to see God's best for each other.

As a single parent, I have found tremendous support in the schools my son has attended. Teachers have kept me in the loop on his performance. I am thankful, because I struggle with the balance between his homework, housework, and other obligations. It helps to know I am not carrying the burden of ensuring his success alone. His father also pushes him with academics as well, because we both value education highly and we want to see him succeed.

As a Christian mom, I have worked at passing on my faith to him since he was in the womb. I have prayed for him, sang to him, and read to him while he was inside, and I continued for a while after he was born. He loves to listen to our local Christian radio station, and he is always fascinated with the stories from the Bible. As an auditory learner, he has fun with my animated storytelling. I pray that the lessons he hears will plant seeds that will take root and grow deep into his heart and life. As a single mom, I have the main responsibility to ensure that his heart is saturated with what we believe, and I take that responsibility seriously.

I want to encourage all single parents who are Christians to seek a family-friendly church. Your children need to grow up with other children whose families share the same faith and moral code. My son is also a good friend with children from school, but my emphasis is typically on family and church friendships. I believe valuable friendships for children makes life more enjoyable and tough times easier to manage. I push harder to help my son make these healthy connections in the absence of his father.

I asked my good friend **Mr. Billie Miller** to share his perspective on parenting his daughter in the form of an interview:

1. **How old was your child when you became a full-time single parent?**
   She was 6 years old.

2. **How long have you been a single parent?**
   At the time of this writing, it has been 10 years.

3. **What were the unique challenges you faced in raising a child alone?**

There were quite a few, but I think one of the biggest ones was a work challenge. My position was being eliminated, but they offered me a better one. However, the new position required that I be to work at 6:00am. With no other parent to help, that was way too early. My employer knew about my situation, but they wouldn't budge on the time. Therefore, I had to make a major decision. I turned down the offer, and I eventually left the job.

4. **Do you feel many of your single-parenting challenges were gender-based (parent or child), especially since you were a father raising a girl?**

   Not really. I thought it would be hard raising my child, especially her being a girl. But it really wasn't. Now don't get me wrong, I'm not saying parenting is easy. But it wasn't as hard as I anticipated.

5. **Were there challenges in navigating schools or any other entity concerning your child?**

   In the beginning it was. When I first got custody of her, I was living in a different school zone from her school. Therefore, her bus didn't come to my neighborhood. I didn't have a car at the time either, so we would ride the city bus to her school, then I would ride it back home. I'd catch the bus back to the school and wait for her outside, then we'd ride it back home together.

6. **Do you feel that your child was at a disadvantage in living with only one parent?**
I think any child is at a disadvantage when living with only one parent, because the family institution was designed for two. But there are different situations that occur to cause a single parent home. Of course with God's help, you can still raise your children up to be successful adults, but the journey will be harder doing it alone.

7. **Any regrets you'd like to share?**
I regret not getting custody of my daughter sooner. Her mother became ill two years before I got custody of her. When this first happened, I was afraid to take on the full-time role. I knew I needed to step up as a father, but I was scared. I didn't know how to be a single parent, especially raising a girl! So that fear caused me to procrastinate. But through much prayer and support, I finally stepped up and got my baby. So if I had to

do it all over again, I would have pursued custody immediately!

8. Any rewards you'd like to share?
My reward is to see my daughter grow. Of course they are kids and they will make mistakes. But when I see her make right decisions or change because of what I taught her, that's my reward. Transformation is my trophy.

"The father of godly children has cause for joy. What a pleasure to have children who are wise." Proverbs 23:24 NLT

9. List 3 key lessons learned in this journey of single parenting.
- STEP UP – I commend all of the strong mothers out there, because for years they've been stepping up. I think mothers almost by nature "step up." Mothers have always stepped up. I think us men can learn from these mothers. It's time for the men to step up. I know that's easier said than done, but we can do it. This was an important lesson for me, because I was dealing with that fear. I was worrying about lack of provision, lack of help, lack of support. I was thinking, *How can I do*

this by myself? But then I got a revelation that nothing was going to show up until I stepped up. I kept asking, "God, how am I going to finish?" God kept asking, "When are you going to start?"

- SHOW UP – It's very important to spend time with your children. This is vital to any parent. Children spell "Love" this way: T-I-M-E. If you want to be a successful parent, you must "show up." They love the money, gifts, and toys, but they love you more. Presents can't take the place of your presence. Show up at the recitals. Show up at the band concerts. Show up at the ball games. From the first day of school to graduation, you need to show up.

- SPEAK UP – You need to open your mouth. You need to speak into your kids' life. And not just a little bit. You need to pour into their life. Don't let the only time they hear you speak to them is when you're correcting them. If the only time that your children hear you talk is when you're fussing at them, then you're not connecting with them.

"Speak up" also involves communication. You need to learn to communicate with your children. Communication is important when it comes to family. When I first got custody of my daughter, we had to do a lot of talking. Communication is a dialogue, not a monologue. In other words, you need to do a lot of talking, but you also need to do a lot of listening. Listen to what your family has to say. Communication is the blood flow that keeps your family alive. Learn to communicate.

10. What advice would you offer to other single parents or to others considering single parenting as a future option?

Get into the presence of God and ask Him to guide you to guide your children. There are many resources that can help you to become a successful parent, but don't forget about the main source—GOD.

No one knows more about a product than the inventor or creator of that product. You wouldn't go to McDonald's and ask them about Burger King's Whopper. You wouldn't go to Toyota and ask them about Ford's vehicles. Likewise, why would you look to the talk shows, soap operas, and therapists before you look to God? He's the Creator of family. So if anybody knows about family, it would be God, the Creator of it. So get into the presence of God and learn from the Creator.

11. Would you recommend single parenting to anyone?

I wouldn't recommend it. Parenting isn't for chumps...especially single parenting. The Scripture speaks about not being prepared for a task in this way:

"Is there anyone here who, planning to build a new house, doesn't first sit down and figure the cost so you'll know if you can complete it? If you only get the foundation laid and then run out of money, you're going to look pretty foolish. Everyone passing by will poke fun at you: 'He started something he couldn't finish.' (Luke 14:28-30, MSG)

For a photo and biography of Billie Miller, refer to the Appendix.

Michelle G. Cameron

Singles Walking into Destiny by Living Intentionally

DO YOU ONLY EXIST, or are you living intentionally with each day that comes? Are we as singles deliberately spending our moments on short-term goals that will only satisfy our current situation, or are we pursuing goals that will allow us to leave a legacy for future generations?

All of us were created to fulfill a purpose. Our Creator has placed a high value on our lives, and so should we. Many of us drift from year to year working in dead-end jobs and going through the same routine every day without asking what can we do to make a difference in the lives of others.

There are many ways that we can ensure we leave our footprint here long after we're gone.

Spiritual Growth

Spiritual growth is the foundation on which all other destiny-related pursuits are built. We may be seeking a deeper relationship with Christ, or we may be new on the Christian journey. Regardless of where we are, we need to consider our spiritual growth and depth over time. If you are a leader (leading a ministry or an appointed/licensed/ordained leader), your spiritual inputs must be significant enough to heal and strengthen you and pour into others as well. Spending time in honest, transparent prayer before God, reading/listening to the Word of God, meditating on Scriptures (with the help of a good commentary), and fasting are regular disciplines of anyone who wants to grow deeply in God. Also consider reading inspirational and spiritually challenging books. Using a daily devotional is highly recommended. Many people also recommend journaling, as this is a great way to capture heartfelt thoughts and experiences to enhance your spiritual journey.

Volunteering

Singles can volunteer for many organizations to give back to those who may be underserved, to expand their network, and to invest in the future generations. Volunteering brings a healthy balance to everyone's lives, where we get the chance to pour into others some of what was poured into us. Whether singles roll up their sleeves to help build a house for the underserved in one weekend get into a soup kitchen serving line, or help a child with homework, volunteering ensures that they practice paying it forward to someone else who is going through a tough situation. Singles with children who are older may consider volunteering with them periodically so they begin to understand the concept of giving back to those who may need assistance.

Donations

If singles do not have the time to spare to volunteer, they can donate items to those who need them. Whether it is clothing no longer needed or basic items that everyone needs, offering a hand up goes a long way.

Some other options to consider are regular monetary donations to non-profit organizations that support causes they are interested in. These donations are typically tax-deductible.

Mentoring/Sponsorships

Singles may offer free tutoring to children or provide internships or sponsorships for college students who want to work in their field of expertise. These are meaningful ways to invest in the future.

Also consider becoming a mentor! This is a rewarding way to pour into the lives of the younger generation and build meaningful, lifelong connections. There are many reputable organizations that offer viable opportunities to mentor others.

Pursue Your Passion

Do you love to write? Do you enjoy speaking? Do you always want to redecorate your home? Do you enjoy cleaning? Are you awesome at organizing events? Does shopping and putting an outfit together cause you to do the happy dance? Maybe it's time to share your love for life with the world. Creativity comes from our Creator. If we make the world a better place with our contributions, we will inspire others to do the same. Take these passions and pursue them as far as you can go with them. Your passion may become your main source of income with time, planning, and mentoring.

Living intentionally includes all the things listed above and so much more. Knowing where you are going and creating a viable plan to take you there is where it all starts. Submit to the process of mentoring and do all the groundwork upfront. Ensure that every business-related venture is properly established to prevent issues later with back-taxes and other violations.

Live with the intention to inspire and encourage. If you happen to be great at what you do, consider offering your expertise to others as a consultant. Support others who are on the journey to discovering their destiny and who don't want to settle for mediocrity. Live to strengthen your lineage and leave a legacy behind for others to follow.

Singles and Mentors

MOST SINGLES THAT I KNOW LIVE LIFE on their terms every day, and few think of being mentored outside of work or volunteer situations. Mentoring can help singles live fulfilled lives and allow them to reach goals that bring satisfaction and achievement. Do you have a mentor to help you navigate through life?

Every successful person has a mentor, such as Paul C Brunson, the renowned matchmaker who partnered with OWN (Oprah's Network) for Lovetown USA. Even mentors have mentors! Mentors push us to be our best and help us reach heights we may have never thought possible.

Some of us have a mentor for each aspect of our lives. Others are blessed to have a mentor who can help them connect and maximize in all major areas of their lives. Whichever situation you are blessed to have, cherish it! Mentors are typically older and wiser than their mentees, but that is not always the case. Today's mentors may be younger but are more successful at whatever goal you are trying to achieve.

When Do I Need A Mentor?

You need a mentor when you feel "stuck" and unsure of how to navigate your way to the next level. You may want to seek ways to refine what you already know to increase productivity. You may want to switch careers or pursue a promotion. You may be launching a new business, or you want to be a better parent. These are some of the instances where you may seek a mentor.

Whom Do I Approach to become My Mentor?

This is where networking comes in. As you interact with people in various settings (whether at a volunteer event, a professional event, or even at a family picnic) you will begin to learn who are experts on certain topics. Observe their success. Try to attend any events they may be hosting or participating in to get a feel for their level of expertise. If you are comfortable, and they display skills or success you desire, approach them and request a mentoring arrangement. They may be flattered by your request and may respond positively. If they are very busy, you may be referred to someone else. Some may mentor for a fee as a life coach, which is definitely a strong option.

Realize that you and your mentor need to be a good fit for the relationship to work. Sometimes finding the right mentor may be a bit of trial and error. Keep at it until you find the right mentoring situation for you.

Mentee Expectations

Typically it is the mentee who schedules the appointments with the mentor based on mutual agreement. Discuss what you hope to gain from the mentoring experience. Determine how long the mentoring arrangement will continue. When the meetings are scheduled, be on time and be specific with what you would like to discuss. Take notes and be prepared to follow up with conversations on how you implemented their suggestions. Mentors expect to see growth and development in their investment; otherwise, it becomes a waste of their time.

Mentor Expectations

As a mentee, you will also have some expectations of your mentor. He or she must come to you with ideas that will help you navigate successfully toward your goal. Each person's situation is unique, so you need a mentor who will look at your situation and offer practical guidance that will enhance or change your personal scenario. A "cookie-cutter" style does not work well in this instance.

Expect your mentor to be able to share "inside" tips on how best to approach situations, typically from their expert knowledge and/or experience. Be open and be willing to follow exactly what they offer or suggest. If you try their suggestion and it did not work for you, plan to discuss it and discover the pros and cons. Allow every step in the development of the relationship to work to your benefit. Learn every lesson the mentor is willing to teach.

Singles Preparing for Marriage

As many of us who may read this book are preparing for marriage, let us remember a few things:

1. Marriage is a covenant between God, man, and woman. It is meant to last until one person dies.

2. Marriage should never be entered into lightly.

3. Ensure you are fully healed before pursuing a relationship, and if you are not yet healed and begin a relationship, consider taking

some time away to process and heal from past pain before moving forward.

4. Don't rush into marriage.

5. Surround yourselves with praying accountability partners who can guide and counsel both of you as you prepare to marry.

6. Spend significant time in prayer and fasting as you prepare to marry. Ask God to show you anything that may be a hindrance in the relationship or to unveil any red flags that could cause serious issues in the marriage.

7. Focus mainly on character than on appearance and physical assets. Should their features change or money disappear, can you still love them and live with them?

8. Choose to fall in love with someone who you can live with and love for a long, long time. Lust is seasonal. Love extends beyond seasons.

9. Marry someone whom you cannot imagine living without.

10. Allow God to write your love story. Don't force anything to happen prematurely, and please do not chase anyone down! Let them choose you freely.

Single By Choice

"But I want you to be without care. He who is unmarried cares for the things of the Lord—how he may please the Lord."
(1 Cor 7:32, NKJV)

I HAVE MET ONLY A FEW PEOPLE who decided to be single by choice versus by circumstance. Many who are single by choice may have decided to be so due to personal experiences such as failed relationships or the death of a beloved partner. Others may just have no desire for marriage and enjoy the freedom that being unmarried brings. I have one relative who is happily single, and I recently lost another relative who chose to live as a single and served the church and local community.

Choosing to be single in a world where sex takes over most of our advertising and media is indeed a gift from God. Choosing to be single may not mean that the person is devoid of sexual urges or temptations, but they have made a conscious decision to remain unattached to a romantic partner.

Many singles in this category move on to have fulfilling careers and offer meaningful contributions to society. I believe that there are many who have made this choice consciously but have not shared it with others for fear of ridicule or accusation of being gay, etc.

I think that singles who have chosen to remain single should feel no shame in telling others of their choice. Your boldness in living life 100 percent on your terms should be applauded. In fact, many may envy the freedom you have for choosing this path. Just think of all you can do and where you can go! I think of missions work or taking time off to help others in your local community just because you can!

My encouragement to you is this: Ensure that you are living out your purpose. Use your time wisely. Inspire others. Allow others to step into your personal world to view your heart and passion. I found that many who decide to live without a mate have much love to give; it's so much that they could not share it with just one person! They passionately pour themselves into others and give to those who are less fortunate. They are typically able to live simply and can decide to pursue any career just because they want to and not necessarily because they have to.

Some who have chosen to live a life of singleness may become involved in relationships but decide not to marry. My concern about that path is that emotional ties may develop and the other party may not understand the "I don't want to get married" aspect of the relationship. For the sake of saving hearts from hurt, choose to remain platonic friends instead.

I admire those who choose to remain single. Thank you for your contributions to the world and to God's Kingdom!

What *Not* To Say To Singles

THE FOLLOWING ARE COMMENTS THAT SINGLES hear from others on their singleness, especially in reference to marriage.

See if you can identify with any of these comments or questions:

1. This is the number one question that singles receive and can be most damaging: "When are you getting married?"

2. "What? Never married? Why not? What's wrong with you?"

3. "We will see how much stuff you're going to do when you get married." (This was in reference to a single woman possibly working after marriage.)

4. "Are you gay?"

5. *"Do you want to be an old maid?"*

6. *"Maybe your standards are too high."*

7. *"Don't get married!" This was said to a woman after she became engaged.*

8. *"You don't want to be married? Do you prefer being alone/single?"*

9. *"Hurry up! You're not getting any younger. What are you waiting for?"*

10. *"So are you reconciling with your ex?" (Question asked of a single parent after a divorce.)*

If you are single, you already understand the angst and frustration many of these questions bring. Somehow, others make it sound as if we have control over when we meet the love of our lives and when we get married.

Some of us, however, do have some issues that we need to address to bring us closer to the point of meeting and being able to handle Mr. Right or Mrs. Right. There may be fears to conquer, financial demons to slay, or other preparations needed before becoming involved with someone else.

When we are asked these questions, let us realize that many are said to us out of concern for our happiness and well-being. Some questions or comments are coming from fear, again out of concern for us. Then others like to see us squirm when we are asked these questions. It is important to maintain an attitude of calmness and respond lovingly and carefully. Let them know how much you are enjoying your singleness and that you have a lot to do to prepare to become a wife or husband. If you do not desire to be in a relationship (in the near future or ever) you may share your thoughts or find a tactful way to let them know it is none of their concern.

Many of these questions are typically coming from older people (like grandparents or mothers in the church). I still believe that there are kind ways to let them know that you are aware of their concern and you will get married as soon as the Lord provides the right person.

Single over the Holidays

This chapter was posted as an article (written by me) on the "Black and Married with Kids" website on December 24, 2013. I would like to share it with you here.

MANY OF US THINK OF THE Thanksgiving, Christmas, and New Year Holidays as "family" holidays. Children who left for college return home to celebrate. Families reunite at Mom and Dad's house as the cousins and siblings exchange gifts, stories, and create warm memories to cherish. During these times singles may feel left out, so here are some ways you can focus on enjoying the holidays while single.. Here are some ways you can focus on enjoying the holidays while single.

1. Spend as much time as possible with family members and close friends over the holiday

season. Accepting invitations for dinner, brunch, parties, and so on should definitely be on the list. Never isolate yourself just because you're single.

2. Get in the holiday spirit! If you love being in the kitchen, try out some holiday recipes that you can share with a group of friends. Go ice-skating, attend a tree-lighting ceremony, go caroling, or create a snowman! Have fun!

3. Host at least one holiday gathering. Consider having a potluck event where everyone brings a dish or dessert. Pop in a holiday-themed DVD for a few laughs (or tears!) as you create amazing memories together!

4. Spend some time window-shopping (or holiday shopping) in village outlets or in the closest large city. The beautiful decorations and joyous atmosphere can bring excitement and happiness to your heart.

5. Make it your priority to enjoy the holidays while single! Share these special moments with those who mean the most to you so you can create amazing memories.

I have learned by personal experience that it is a choice for me to regret being single during the holidays vs. going out and creating a new life. For example, last year (2013) I was invited by a family to spend Thanksgiving with them. They have an annual tradition of each person sharing a Scripture verse at the table after the Thanksgiving blessing. That was a blessed experience for me to have, and I will always treasure that holiday invitation.

I encourage you to make that effort to do something different for the next holiday! Create a memory, or start a new tradition!

Single and Free! *Final Words*

Being single is not a death sentence. Instead, look at your singleness as a season of preparation. Prepare yourself mentally, emotionally, spiritually, financially, physically, and practically for marriage. Enjoy the journey on your way there. Allow the process to take its course. That moment when we feel we've arrived, we may find that there are other things we can work on.

Love yourself. Be kind to yourself. Allow yourself to enjoy your life right where you are. Sometimes we torture ourselves because we live in regret or wish we had what someone else has. Looking at life in this way does not make it easier to be single. Wishing we had a relationship like Mary and Joe does not help us, because we do not know what is happening in that relationship behind closed doors. We only see what they allow us to see. We may not want what they have when we find out the details.

Lavish on yourself. I speak especially to our single parents. Many of us are sacrificing a lot to raise our children, and some of us are not receiving any type of support from the other parent for whatever reason. Whenever we get free moments, let us use that time to relax and pursue whatever replenishes us. Find a way to save toward a short vacation or a spa treatment or just plan to enjoy time away from the typical routine. Learning to laugh and enjoy life makes it easier to face daily challenges and difficulties.

Work through your pain. Any pain that we hang on to over time becomes comfortable. We should never want our hearts to get used to feeling pain every day, all the time. Pain is the signal that something is wrong. As it is in our natural bodies, so it is in our emotions and spirits. Working through pain may be the hardest thing any of us will ever do, but the benefits are priceless. Our overall outlook on life improves significantly, and our bodies are more relaxed and healed when we remove the source of pain from our lives. Allow the presence of God to minister to you in the recesses of your heart and mind. Healing is available for everyone who craves it.

Fix your life. Be relentless about getting better in every area of life. Challenge yourself. Make yourself uncomfortable at least once a week. Stretching yourself often makes life interesting and leaves you feeling fulfilled. The comfort zone has many graves. Don't allow your life to become stagnant and boring. Visit new places alone or with friends. Wear something that is not your typical look. Learn a new language or about a new culture. Take a class or pursue another degree. Give a speech in front of an audience. Whatever you do, don't live and die without experiencing life!

Teach someone else. Find someone else to pour your lessons into. Let them know how you made it, and share what else you are doing to continue making it. This person must be someone who is worth your time and attention. Allow your wisdom to teach them how to avoid some of life's pitfalls and traps and how to handle challenges. You have something to leave behind, even if you are not a biological parent. Share your knowledge!

Allow only God to define you. Don't allow jobs, bosses, family, friends, or enemies to define you! You are made in the image of God, after His likeness. He placed you on this earth to fulfill amazing things. Take your life definition from the One with the blueprint for who you are and what you are to become. The confines of others push many of us into mediocrity. Don't allow others to box you in!

Singles – Questions for Reflection

These questions are based on the content in this book. Use them as a guide for self-assessment and refining personal challenge areas where needed. Let's go!

1. You're single. Now what? List three things you need to do to enhance your life so it can be all that you desire it to be.

2. Reflect on your past and present romantic life. Are there soul ties? If so, seek the help of a pastor or a mental health professional to guide you toward healing. I also recommend this article *"She Didn't Steal Your Man; He Was Already Hers In the Spirit"* by Linda Grosvenor Holland. (http://lovebetterinstitute.com/she-didnt-steal-your-man-he-was-already-hers-in-the-spirit/)

3. Are you fully aware of the times when you are most vulnerable sexually? What two steps do you take to help you stay sexually pure?

4. List three things you will do to clearly define boundaries between you and friends of the opposite sex.

5. What five things are you doing to improve your health in every way? Include mental health in your list.

6. Do you have a working budget? If not, contact Kenny Pugh to get a budget overview to help you review the challenge areas for spending control.

7. If you are a single parent who needs support or encouragement, feel free to contact me directly via email. I would like to build a network to help all of us as we raise our children.

8. List two things to work on this year to help you walk into your purpose/destiny.

9. Do you have a mentor? You need one if you expect to grow in any area of your life. Pray about it and ask God to direct you to someone.

10. What new tradition can you add to your holiday celebrations?

11. What three things are you working on to prepare for marriage?

12. If you are choosing to remain single, what are your life goals, and what are your plans for future long-term care and final arrangements, as shared in the Singles and Finances chapter? Even if you plan to marry, these are important items to consider and put in place.

13. What did you learn from this book? Feel free to share your comments with the author or on media outlets!

Social Media Quotes for Singles

Below are a few of my social media posts that apply to singles. In fact, my series of postings printed below birthed this book!

The intent of including these posts is to start meaningful and interesting conversations and push us to where we need to be, spiritually and otherwise. Enjoy!

Just a thought: Many times we are afraid of choosing (or accepting) the one whom God has designed for us because they may be different from our original preference (whether ethnicity, body type, financial status, etc). There's nothing wrong with giving a friendship time to develop, but after enough time has passed and personal assessments have been made, allow God show you who the person really is and go with His affirmation.

After you've prayed, spoken to accountability partners, read the Word, interacted with the person, talked to mutual friends, and put them through myriads of tests, a decision needs to be made. Let God help you decide, and don't be afraid to confirm what God has already shown you on many days in many ways.

Only God knows the end from the beginning. Take that leap of faith, my friends! You'll be glad you did! **(Nov 29, 2013)**

There is a crippling spirit of "unavailability" that is endemic among singles. Many are unavailable because their hearts are tied to someone they are not in a relationship with. Others are unavailable because they aren't healed from past relationships. Then there's the group of singles who won't commit to just one person. Let's get this right in 2014! Let's unburden and unyoke ourselves so that we are available for all that God has in store for us. **(Dec 30, 2013)**

(Jan 1, 2014)

1. Sleeping with him is NOT a commitment.

2. Living with him is NOT a commitment.

3. If a man cannot live without you, he will ask you to marry him.

4. Do you pray for others often/daily? This is a preview of what your marriage will be!

5. Setting healthy boundaries includes saying "no" without needing a lengthy explanation.

6. Are you flexible? Can you be spontaneous? These are desirable traits to bring into marriage!

7. The art of listening without preparing a response in your mind = priceless (I'm still working on this…)

8. Love yourself first before attempting to love someone else.

9. Pretending to be what you are not eventually wears off. It is impossible to fool everyone forever.

10. Are you nice to others only when you want something from them? This is a preview of what your marriage will look like….

11. Do you care about your appearance at all times? Is hygiene high on your list? Please note that this is a preview of what your marriage will look like.

12. Can you communicate after a disagreement, or do you get silent and ignore him or her? This is a preview of what your marriage will look like.

13. Can you keep on loving, serving, and helping even when you're not in the mood or when you do not feel well? This is a preview of what your marriage will look like.

14. Can you make any kind of commitment and stick with it? That's a preview of what your marriage will look like.

15. Question: Ladies, do you maintain an atmosphere of peace wherever you are? Husbands want to come home to a peaceful atmosphere.

16. If only one person is committed, you are not in a relationship.

17. Being a gentleman is extremely attractive.

18. Marriage is ministry on steroids!

19. If we are looking to marry to see what we can get, then our focus is wrong. The main focus in

a healthy marriage is giving/serving each other. You should plan on out-serving each other!

21. No man or woman can satisfy us or please us in every way. We are all human. Only God can do it!

22. No husband or wife can take loneliness away.

23. Maintaining your focus on your God-given purpose brings fulfillment.

24. Your heart can only receive if it is ready.

25. Waiting on God to send your spouse does NOT include staying in your house by the phone, waiting on a man to call you! What are you working on? Are you pursuing your purpose? Do you have more degrees to study for? Are you helping those who cannot help themselves (volunteering, etc.)? What are you doing while you wait?

26. Single men, ask yourself this question: "Can I live without her?"

27. Not every person you attract (or you are attracted to) is meant for you to pursue or to date. Pray for discernment before you respond

to attraction. It could be fatal to your destiny and can literally cost you your life!

28. Ladies, it is out of God's order for us to pursue men. When we chase, we will have to continue the chase for the rest of the relationship. Being pursued works in our favor.

29. Sometimes we've already met "the one" for us, but we are still a work in progress. It's not yet time. Are you willing to continue working on you and wait?

30. Sisters, when you are actively pursuing peace with everyone while getting rid of hate, soul ties, and negative thoughts, you are becoming more attractive to the man whom God has handpicked for you. As you work on building up yourself and getting healed, you will stand out. Never stoop low enough to fight another woman for a man's attention.

31. Singles, ask yourself this question: "Why do I want to marry?"

32. Sisters, our hearts will always shine through. If our hearts are filled with hate, bitterness, and pain, our countenance and behavior will reflect this. If we are filled with Jesus's joy, our faces

will glow and our lives will be impacted for God and His Kingdom everywhere we go.

33. To all my single ladies: We want the single men to make a choice, but are we ready to be wives? Have we invested in our hearts, spirits, and minds as much as (or more than) we've invested on our appearance? Husbands need to know that we are more than just pretty faces.

34. Do you practice "tit for tat" or payback when you are wronged? This is a preview of what your marriage will look like.

(Jan 5, 2014)

1. God may bring our spouse to us and we may say, "That's not them!" Are you willing to look beyond your personal preferences and look at their character?

2. Are you prepared to love them even if they never change?

3. If you love someone, be prepared to love the unlovely aspects of who they are as well.

4. Real love COVERS. Are you being covered? Or are you being exposed to others?

5. Trust plays a major role in love relationships. Can I trust you? I also want you to know that you can trust me.

6. Don't fool yourself into thinking that marriage is a cure for any personal deficiency you are struggling with now. Marriage sometimes amplifies issues.

7. Make finding your "why" your main focus. In God's time He will bring someone to walk with you toward your destiny.

8. Don't fix your life just to get a spouse. Remember that the real work begins after the wedding ends!

9. Are we really in love, or are we in love with the idea of love? Real Love = Patience + Sacrifice/Selflessness

10. Are you prepared to love them even if they never change?

11. Look at WHY you do what you do. Is it because you want to do it, or is it because someone else is expecting it? Or are you trying to impress others?

12. Lesson Learned: You cannot work for love. Someone will love you for you. Don't forget God's example!

I've learned that many may view you in terms of how you can fit into their plans. If you are not careful, you can say "yes" to something that God did not intend for you because of the desire to please others. **(Jan 6, 2014)**

(Jan 8, 2014)

1. Singles: It is not the woman's role to give a man vision. He must be already equipped with his God-given vision and actively working toward it. A woman's role is to help the man birth his vision. She is his help-meet.

   Men: If you do not have vision, you do not need help.

2. Many singles desire to be married, but if you are unwilling to be flexible or to grow and change, you are better off single.

3. Remember that being single is NOT a curse! It's time for growth and a bit of fun too!

4. Be yourself! Never try to change who you are to impress anyone.

5. I've learned to compete only with myself. Making myself uncomfortable at least once a week works wonders. Try it!

6. How do you make yourself uncomfortable? Push yourself to perform a task that will force you to grow, whether it's socially, mentally, educationally, physically, spiritually, financially, or all of the above!

7. Are we satisfied with struggling every day just to have a decent lifestyle? Are we willing to push ourselves to do better today so that the struggle can be minimized tomorrow?

8. Is your perspective on life exactly the same as it was ten years ago or one year ago? Have you grown?

9. It amazes me how many of us allow years to pass by without making any significant changes! We've grown older but not wiser!

Reflecting today... A family will never grow higher than the head. If the head of the household isn't a visionary who is willing to put in the work and show the way, then the family cannot be expected to achieve its highest goals. Ladies, please keep this in mind when deciding who to marry. **(Jan 13, 2014)**

(Feb 2, 2014)

1. Singles, are you accountable to spiritual leadership while dating? Do you think it is necessary to "check in" with someone else about your love life?

2. Can your significant other cover you spiritually? Can they do spiritual warfare on your behalf? Can you wrestle in the spirit on their behalf?

3. What need or desire is your significant other fulfilling in your life? What need or desire are you fulfilling in their life? Ask yourself these questions.

4. If the person you're with now became seriously ill or permanently disabled or disfigured, would you stay with them?

5. Why do you want to marry? What's the real reason? Ask yourself this question.

Special Thanks

I would like to thank God for being my strength to do all that I do every day—Mommy, leader, and the other hats I wear. I also thank my church family and social media friends who encourage me to keep writing! Thank you for reading and interacting with me online whenever you can. I also want to thank my mentors and close circle that help me see the areas where I can grow and spread my wings. I am truly grateful. Last (but not least) I want to thank my family for their continuous support and encouragement. I've dared to share my heart and life on paper, and they have stood by me. THANK YOU!

Appendix

Biographical Sketch

Joshua Peters Smith is an anointed man of God with a mandate to cultivate and empower a Joshua Generation of believers, helping them to find their purpose, reach their destiny, and maximize their full potential. Called "A prophetic voice to the nation for this generation," Prophet Joshua has been preaching over thirteen years and has devoted most of his life to the work of the ministry.

Professionally, Joshua holds a bachelor's degree in psychology, a master's degree in professional counseling, and is currently pursuing a Ph.D. in psychology. Joshua has over five years' experience in the mental health field and is currently pursuing LPC licensure in the state of Mississippi. At the time of publication, Joshua will have received credentials as a Certified Mental Health Therapist.

Prophet Joshua is also an entrepreneur, musician, mentor, a certified life coach, and the acclaimed author of *Dream Again: The Journey toward Destiny*.
For coaching opportunities, email Joshua at joshuapeterssmith@gmail.com or call 601-336-0614.

About the Contributor:

Kenny Pugh is a strategist, coach, author of *Can You Do It Standing Up?*, speaker, media personality, sought-after speaker on finances, singleness, relationships, and life. He is also the visionary behind KTP Financial, LLC (www.ktpfinancial.com). You can find more information about Kenny at www.kennypugh.com.

Singles and Finances reference:
[(Rank, M. R. (2011, Spring). Rethinking american poverty. *Contexts, 10*, 16-21. doi:http://dx.doi.org/10.1177/1536504211408794].

Couple and Family Psychology: Research and Practice, 2(2), 131-145. doi:http://dx.doi.org/10.1037/a0032025).

BILLIE MILLER *"The Motivational Minister"* is a Bible teacher, speaker, and the #1 Amazon Bestselling Author of *Life in Righteousness: The Word is Your Life* and *30 Days of Righteousness: The Word is Your Life Action Plan*. Thousands of lives have been changed through Billie's powerful teachings. For more information, please visit www.BillieMiller.com.

Contact the Author

Website: www.michellegcameron.com

Blog: www.michellegcameronwrites.com

Twitter: https://twitter.com/ShellyLove2002

Instagram: http://instagram.com/shellylove2002

Facebook: https://www.facebook.com/MichelleGCameronLLC

LinkedIn: Michelle G. Cameron

Email: michellegcameron@gmail.com

Mail: P.O. Box 1693, Piscataway NJ 08855-1693

Other titles from the Author: *It's My Life and I Live Here: One Woman's Story* (NyreePress). Available in eBook format everywhere eBooks are sold.

Michelle G. Cameron is available for speaking engagements, individual or group coaching/ consultations, and assisting singles ministries everywhere as requested. Please contact her for details at michellegcameron@gmail.com.

NyreePress

NyreePress Literary Group
"Publishing Life for Families"

WWW.NYREEPRESS.COM

WWW.BUGLOVEBOOKS.COM

Twitter: @nyreepress

www.ingramcontent.com/pod-product-compliance
Lightning Source LLC
Chambersburg PA
CBHW072058290426
11110CD00011B/1725